GOLF

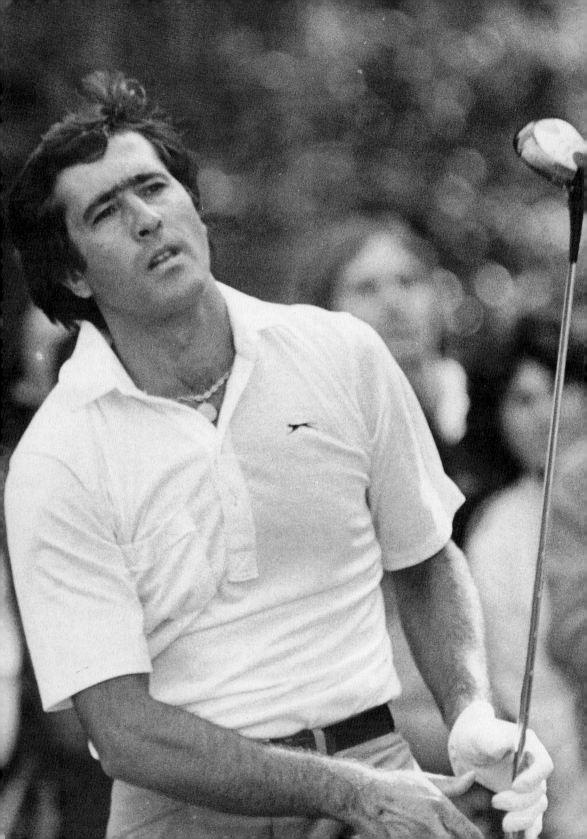

PLAY THE GAME

GOLF

IAN MORRISON

BLANDFORD

First published in Great Britain in 1988
by Ward Lock. Revised and updated
by Blandford, Wellington House, 125 Strand,
London WC2R 0BB
A Cassell Imprint

Reprinted 1994 (twice), 1996

Designed by Anita Ruddell
Illustrations by Peter Bull Art

Text set in Helvetica
Printed and bound in Great Britain by
The Bath Press, Avon

British Library Cataloguing in Publication Data

Morrison, Ian, 1947–
   Play the game : golf.
   1. Gold – Manuals
   I. Title
   796.352'3

ISBN 0 7137 2442 0

Acknowledgments

The author and publishers would like to
thank Colorsport for supplying the
photographs reproduced in this book.

Cover: **Greg Norman fires an iron shot from
light rough at Wentworth in 1992. The
Australian showed himself to have retained
his winning game when he triumphed in the
1993 British Open.**

CONTENTS

FOREWORD

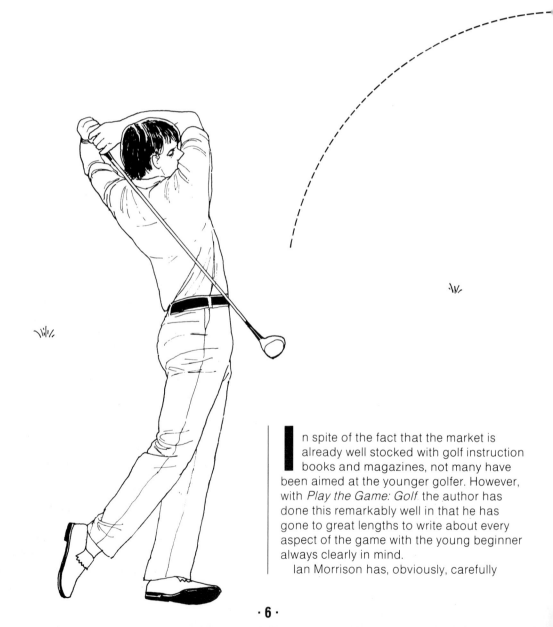

In spite of the fact that the market is already well stocked with golf instruction books and magazines, not many have been aimed at the younger golfer. However, with *Play the Game: Golf* the author has done this remarkably well in that he has gone to great lengths to write about every aspect of the game with the young beginner always clearly in mind.

Ian Morrison has, obviously, carefully

FOREWORD

researched his subject, particularly with regard to the origin of the game and the original equipment used by our predecessors. The book leads the reader through into the equipment required for present-day golf and the everyday terminology used in the playing of the game.

There is also considerable merit in the way that the author has set about providing the reader with a clear picture of the rules, and I particularly like the way in which he has presented them in the form of questions and answers in the 'Rules Clinic'.

The section on technique is based on sound fundamentals, and any golf swing built on these lines will be both effective and durable. Ian Morrison has played safe by sticking to tried and tested principles and has not yielded to the temptation of introducing any obscure theories. I am impressed by the way in which he has carefully aimed his text at those players who need clear instruction most of all – young novices. *Play the Game: Golf* is therefore a welcome and valuable addition to the ever-growing body of literature on how to play golf.

John Stirling
National Coach English Golf Union and
Senior Instructor PGA Training School
P.G.A. Captain 1989
Consultant to the Golf Foundation

HISTORY &

DEVELOPMENT OF

GOLF

Over the years many attempts have been made to establish the origins of golf. Scotland is regarded as the 'home of golf' but it is doubtful that the game was first played there.

A link between golf and a game called *paganica* has been found. *Paganica* was introduced into Britain by the Romans. A later form of this game, *cambuca* was seen in Britain in the fourteenth century. Played with a bent stick and wooden ball, it certainly bore a resemblance to the game of today.

The word golf is possibly derived from either the German word *kolbe* meaning club, or the Dutch derivation *kolf*. Some antique prints show the Dutch playing a game with curved sticks and a round ball with a hole as a target.

The first conclusive evidence of golf being played in Britain was in 1457, when a statute was passed banning the playing of golf in Scotland because it interfered with archery practice and thus, indirectly, was a threat to the nation's defence. The Scottish Parliament put out a proclamation in 1471 which said: '*That in na place of the realme there be usit futteballis, golfe, or other sik unprofitabele sportis for the common gude of the realme*' . . . in other words pack in playing football and golf – or else! For such a proclamation to be issued the game *must* have been popular in Scotland at the time; thus even if golf was not born in Scotland, evidence suggests that here was its first stronghold in Britain.

By the end of the fifteenth century the sport had regained its popularity, even though men were convicted for playing golf on Sundays rather than attending church. Some vicars still have the same problem today!

The game was, however, becoming well established north of the border, and two Scottish kings, James IV and James V, both played at East Lothian. Mary Queen of Scots, a dab hand at most sports, is said to have been playing golf at St Andrews at the time of the murder of her second husband Darnley, in 1567. For many historians, this has merely added fuel to the belief that she had something to do with his murder – a round of golf would have provided a very good alibi!

Golf was certainly a game for royalty and nobility at that time; Mary's son, James I of England, took the game south and is believed to have played at Blackheath. Both Charles I and Charles II enjoyed a round of golf and an old print depicts Charles I playing at Leith when a messenger arrived with the news of the impending Irish rebellion . . . I suppose Charles was the Francis Drake of the golf world!

However, in England the game was not as well organized as in Scotland, and Royal Blackheath was one of its few outposts. North of the border however, it was a different matter. The game, although without unified rules, was being played in many parts of Scotland. The first steps towards developing golf into the game as it is known today were in 1744 when the sport's first club, the Honourable Company of Edinburgh Golfers, was formed on 1 May, with William St Clair of Roselin its first captain.

The Honourable Company were based at Leith and played over a five-hole course. They later moved to Musselburgh before settling at their present-day home at Muirfield in 1891. The club members decided to organize their own competition, and in order to see fair play a set of thirteen rules was drawn up.

Following the formation of the Honourable Company other clubs were born, each with their own sets of rules. The most notable new club was the Royal and Ancient at St Andrews in 1754 when, on 14 May, twenty-two noblemen and gentlemen of Fife formed themselves into 'The Society of St Andrews Golfers'.

Other important developments began to take place, notably in the manufacture of the ball. Early balls were almost certainly made of wood, but when the game developed in Scotland they were made from a leather case stuffed with feathers. One top hat full of feathers was required for each ball. Not surprisingly these balls were known as 'featheries'. A good craftsman could make *four* 'featheries' in a day.

In the middle of the nineteenth century a new substance, gutta percha, a gum extracted from a Malayan tree, was being used for the insulating of cables. An employee of the company that made these cables applied the substance to a golf ball and tried his new ball out at Blackheath. The main advantage was its durability. It was cheaper and far less destructable than the feathery but, being solid, if not hit properly it

The feathery

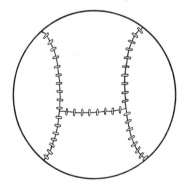

The guttie

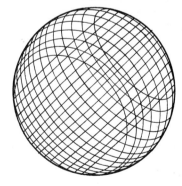

In the middle of the 19th century the guttie replaced the feathery. While it retained its round shape, the ball was solid and if hit awkwardly would jar the player's elbow or arm.

gave a nasty jar to the arm. However, the 'featheries' were soon replaced on a mass scale.

At this time there were no organized competitions, other than within clubs themselves, and the main form of competition was between players of rival clubs and consisted of money matches over a pre-determined number of holes and often over each of the players' courses.

The 'champion' of the day was Allan Robertson, and it was on his death in 1859 that the Prestwick Golf Club decided to run an open competition to find out who Robertson's successor was to be. That competition was the world's first golf tournament – the British Open. Today, it remains the most famous tournament in the world.

On Wednesday, 17 October 1860 eight of the best golfers assembled at Prestwick for the first championship. It was played over three rounds of the twelve-hole course. The first winner was Willie Park, who posted a thirty-six-hole total of 174. His prize was a beautiful Moroccan leather belt which, the rules of the competition stipulated, would become the permanent property of any man winning the title three times.

The first championship was inappropriately named because the field consisted of eight professionals and consequently was not an 'open' event. Amateurs of the day protested, and the following year it was a truly 'open' competition. That year one of the game's giants, Old Tom Morris, won by four shots from Park, and in 1862 his winning margin was thirteen strokes, a record which still stands more than 120 years later.

Tom's son, Young Tom, followed his father as champion, and in 1870 he won the Open for the third time and consequently was allowed to keep the championship belt. In the absence of a trophy, the championship was not held in 1871. When it returned the following year the prize was the magnificent claret jug, which is the winner's prize today –

together with a healthy cheque. The new trophy was donated by the Prestwick club, the Royal and Ancient, and the Honourable Company of Edinburgh Golfers. Those three clubs were jointly responsible for the organization of the championship, and it was played at their courses in rotation. Those three courses, like all that have staged the British Open, are links courses – that is, they are sited on the coast.

Golf began to develop south of the border in the 1880s after its slow start, and in 1894 the first Open was held in England. J.H. Taylor, the first English professional to win the title, won at Sandwich. That win heralded the start of a twenty-year period which would be dominated by three men; J.H. Taylor, James Braid, and Harry Vardon. Between them they became known as 'The Great Triumvirate', and won the British Open no less than sixteen times between 1894 and 1914.

The Haskell ball

What the inside of a present-day golf ball looks like.

In 1902, in the United States, there came about a notable change in ball manufacture. Coburn Haskell, of the Goodrich Tyre and Rubber Company in Ohio, produced a ball that consisted of rubber strips wound round a rubber core. This new ball became known as the 'Haskell' ball . . . what else could it be called! Shortly before the 1902 British Open the qualities of the Haskell ball were disputed and the 'Great Triumvirate' refused to acknowledge it, but after Sandy Herd outdrove Vardon to win the title it soon became popular and replaced the 'guttie'.

By the end of the nineteenth century golf had spread throughout Britain and more competitions were taking place. The Scots had a great influence on the development of the game in the United States during the 1880s, as many emigrated and took the game with them. As a result, the first US Open was held over the nine-hole Newport Rhode Island Club in October 1895. It was won by the English-born professional, Horace Rawlins.

Golf had been played in America before this, for as early as 1795 the *Georgia Gazette* made reference to the Savannah Golf Club. But it was not until the Scots invasion in the latter part of the nineteenth century that it achieved the popularity it held in Britain.

One man who could lay claim to arousing interest in the game in America was a Mr Lockhart. He returned to New York from his native Dunfermline armed with a golf bag and balls in 1887 and that year was arrested for hitting golf balls in Central Park. But that led to fellow Scots getting together with Lockhart and forming the first recognized club in the United States – the St Andrews Club at Yonkers, New York. The game received a boost in the latter part of the century when Scottish craftsmen (ball and club makers) emigrated to the States, and in 1900 the game received its biggest possible boost when Harry Vardon competed in, and won, the US Open by beating fellow Briton J.H. Taylor at Chicago.

While Britain and the United States were becoming the strongholds of golf, just as they are today, the game had spread to other parts of the world. The Calcutta Golf Club was founded in India in 1829, France had the first club on the continent of Europe, at Pau in 1856 and in 1870 Australia's first club, at Adelaide, was formed. New Zealand soon followed suit, as did Canada, and then South Africa, Hong Kong and Thailand.

As the game developed, so did golf equipment. The steel shafted club soon replaced the hickory shaft and this feature was to revolutionize the game as much as the rubber-core ball did. Greater lengths were being achieved and it was not long before factory-made clubs were being developed. This virtually made the craftsmen redundant, but some remained, and still exist today. The more the Americans played the game, the more scientific it became, and the British players were forced to follow suit.

British golfers had ruled the world since

Clubs of old

This is what irons looked like in the 18th century.

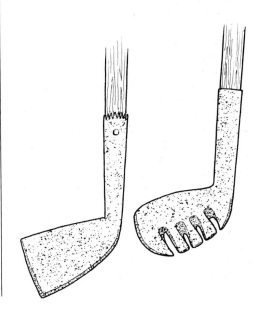

the inauguration of championship golf, but in 1913 a twenty-year-old coachman's son changed the course of golfing history at Brookline, Massachusetts. Francis Ouimet, an amateur who lived over the road from the Brookline course, competed in his first US Open and found himself in a three-way play-off for the title with the top Britons Harry Vardon and Ted Ray. To everyone's amazement, the youngster came out on top. From that day the English were no longer invincible at home or abroad. That victory opened the floodgates, and you will need few reminders of how dominant United States players have been in the golfing world ever since.

Walter Hagen became the first of the great American champions. Flamboyant and extrovert, he brought a new life to the game. He made it fun, and his show business style, on and off the golf course, attracted as much publicity as the Hollywood stars of the day. Hagen's great rival of the 1920s was a Georgian lawyer, Bobby Jones, perhaps the greatest golfer of all time.

Jones never turned professional, but he was capable of beating any man. In 1930 he completed the most remarkable Grand Slam, the like of which will never be repeated. He won the US and British Open championships, as well as winning the amateur titles of both countries, and all within four months of each other.

Since then many great names have graced golf courses the world over. The second 'Great Triumvirate' arrived in the 1940s, when Ben Hogan, Sam Snead and Byron Nelson proved invincible, just as their successors, Arnold Palmer, Gary Player and Jack Nicklaus, did in the 1960s. However, Britain's Tony Jacklin showed in 1969-70 that British golf should never be underestimated, when he won the British

and US Open within twelve months.

In the 1980s, the emergence of such great European players as Severiano Ballesteros, Bernhard Langer, Sandy Lyle and Nick Faldo have caused the pendulum to swing back to British/European domination, as recent European successes in the Ryder Cup have shown.

The ruling body of the game is the Royal and Ancient at St Andrews, which is recognized by most countries except the United States. But the US Golf Association (founded 1894), works very closely with the R & A, who have acted as the authoritative body on the rules of golf since 1897, and over the years more and more countries have turned to the R & A for guidance. The rules committee meets regularly to discuss and review the rules if deemed necessary.

Professional golfers in Britain and the United States are members of their own Professional Golfers Associations. The British PGA was formed in London in 1901 and was the idea of the leading professional of the day, J.H. Taylor. In 1971 the British PGA joined forces with the European Golf Association to form the European PGA Tour, which organizes season long events across Europe. The Open Championship, however, is still under the auspices of the R & A.

The US PGA was founded in 1916 and like their European counterparts organize season-long events for members. Both the European and US Tours restrict the number of players who gain automatic entry to competitions and at the end of the season have a Tour qualifying school for the lower-ranked professionals.

Professional women golfers in Europe and the United States also have their own Tours, and there are now Senior Tours for male professionals over the age of fifty. Many men on these tours are now winning far

Jack Nicklaus here displaying uncharacteristic elation after a great victory in the 1970 British Open at St Andrews. Nicklaus' achievements are unparalleled in the world of golf; he lays a strong claim to being the greatest player of all time.

more money than they ever did in their regular tour days.

Golf is a great game to play and watch. Television has brought the game's big names into the living room. When you first play golf you will realize how hard the game really is. Ballesteros, Nicklaus and Woosnam don't give that impression, but try hitting a little ball into a not-much-bigger hole a quarter of a mile away, and in only four shots . . . that's when you find out how difficult it is.

Golf is not, as many people have imagined over the years, an expensive game to play. Of course it can be if you go out and buy the most expensive set of clubs you can find and become a member of the most exclusive golf club in your area. However, if you want to learn the game, municipal courses charge a moderate green fee, and can even hire you a set of clubs if you don't have your own. Most golf clubs have a resident professional who gives coaching lessons, and you are well advised to invest in a session with a professional before you embark on your first 'solo' round of golf.

Once you have played this great game, which is enjoyed by people of all ages the world over, there is every chance the 'bug' will bite and you will soon want to acquire your own clubs and play regularly. Beware though, the courts are full of wives seeking divorces because they have become 'golf widows' . . .!

EQUIPMENT &
TERMINOLOGY

Golf is played on a grassland area known as a course. It normally constitutes eighteen holes, although some smaller courses may only have nine, twelve or fifteen holes. Championship golf is never played over anything but an eighteen-hole course which normally measures between 6–7000yd (5486–6400m) in length. Each hole is different in length, but each consists of three distinctive areas; the teeing ground, the fairway and the green. Hazards loom for the wayward ball from tee to green; these may take the form of bunkers, out of bounds areas or water hazards. In addition, part of the course is deliberately not cut close, and this is known as the rough.

Teeing ground

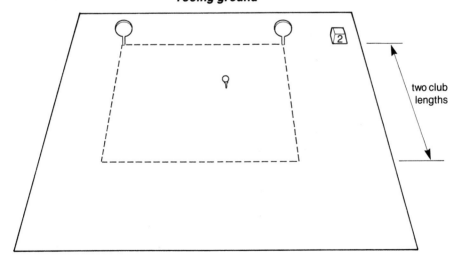

two club
lengths

You may tee your ball up anywhere between the two markers and behind them up to two club-lengths away. The markers are moved periodically to prevent damage to the teeing ground.

GOLF

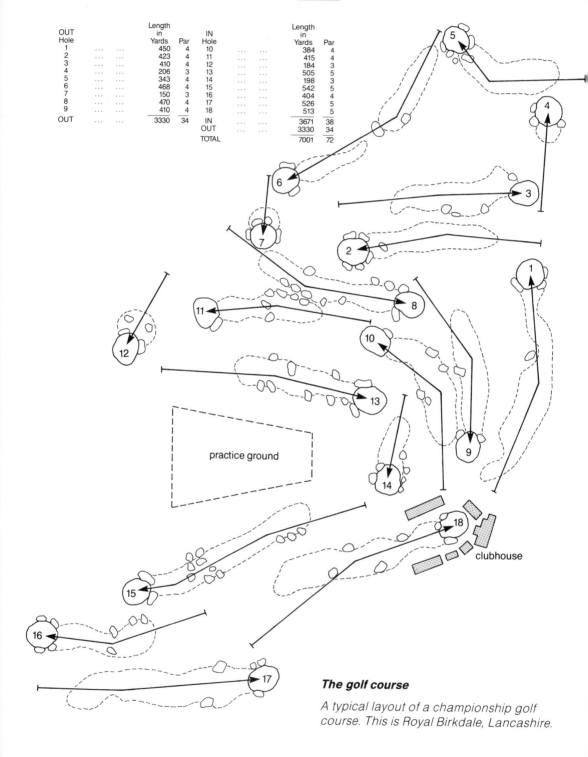

OUT Hole			Length in Yards	Par	IN Hole			Length in Yards	Par
1	...	...	450	4	10	...	...	384	4
2	...	...	423	4	11	...	...	415	4
3	...	...	410	4	12	...	...	184	3
4	...	...	206	3	13	...	...	505	5
5	...	...	343	4	14	...	...	198	3
6	...	...	468	4	15	...	...	542	5
7	...	...	150	3	16	...	...	404	4
8	...	...	470	4	17	...	...	526	5
9	...	...	410	4	18	...	...	513	5
OUT	...	...	3330	34	IN	...	...	3671	38
					OUT	...	...	3330	34
					TOTAL			7001	72

practice ground

clubhouse

The golf course

A typical layout of a championship golf course. This is Royal Birkdale, Lancashire.

The object of the game is simple, even though the practical side of the game may not be, and that is to hit the ball into a hole situated within each of the eighteen (or whatever number) greens by using one or more clubs, each designed for a specific purpose on the golf course.

Let's look first of all at the playing area, the golf course.

The teeing ground

Normally a rectangular piece of land, the teeing ground is often slightly elevated. It is from this area, and this area alone, that you play your first shot at each hole.

Markers are positioned on each teeing area and you must play from between those markers, and behind them up to a maximum distance of two club-lengths away. A box, or marker board, will indicate what number hole you are playing, what the par for the hole is, and how many yards/metres it is to the hole.

Ladies have their own tees, which are forward of the men's, while a third teeing area is set aside for use during competitions.

The fairway

The fairway is the area of cut grass in between the teeing area and the green. It is not cut as short as the green, but is not left to grow so long that you would lose a ball in it. When playing a ball off the fairway you must always replace any divots you take with your club when playing a shot.

The green

This is the area which you are aiming to reach before you eventually put the ball into the hole. The green is manicured and cut

A typical hole, showing the teeing area (a), fairway (b) and putting green (c). Fairway bunkers, greenside bunkers and a water hazard are also present.

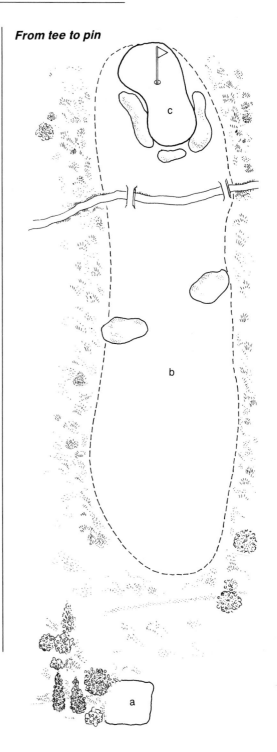

From tee to pin

The green

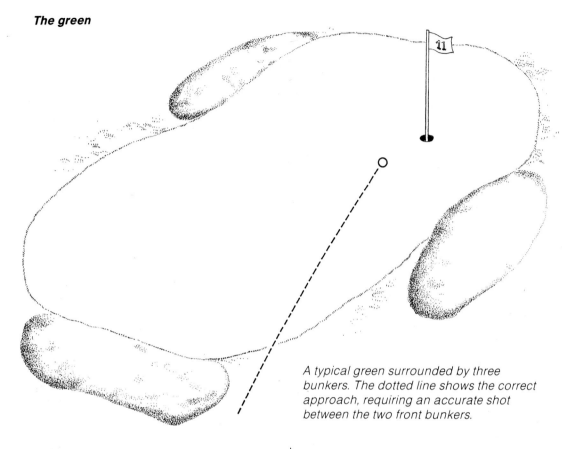

A typical green surrounded by three bunkers. The dotted line shows the correct approach, requiring an accurate shot between the two front bunkers.

very finely to enable fluent and accurate running of the ball. Greens can vary in size and are not always, if ever, completely flat. They have their own peculiarities, and if you play the same course regularly you should try and remember the good and bad parts of the green to play from. Some greens are split level.

In the winter months, most courses will create temporary greens, whereby the groundsman will create a rough green on the fairway to prevent damage being caused to the normal greens in adverse weather conditions. The temporary greens will not be as good as the proper ones and will often be considerably smaller. The only alternative, however, is to close the course during the winter months, but once you have become a golf addict, that is the last thing you would want!

The hole

The eventual target . . . the hole. It can be placed anywhere on the green. It is $4\frac{1}{4}$in (10·79cm) diameter and has a drop of at least 4in (10·16cm). If there is a lining on the inside of the hole, and there is on most of them, it must be sunk at least 1in (2·5cm) below the surface of the green.

A flagstick is a movable round stick placed in each hole to indicate to the players the position of the hole within the green. It normally has a flag on top of it, often bearing the number of the hole. The rules do not stipulate the height of the stick, but it is

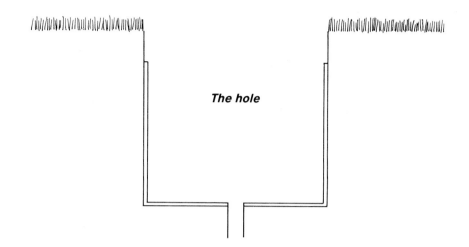

The hole

generally between 5–6ft (1·52–1·83m) in length.

For long holes where the green cannot be sighted from the teeing area, a marker will be placed on the fairway indicating in which direction you should play your shot. The marker will be out of your driving range, so there is little danger of your ball hitting it.

Well, that all sounds nice and easy doesn't it? All you have to do is put your ball on the teeing area, hit it onto the fairway and then onto the green (or straight onto the green if it is a short hole). After that, all you have to do is hit the ball into the hole. Don't kid yourself though – there is a lot more to it than that. Make the slightest error with your tee shot and you could find yourself in all sorts of trouble.

You most probably have the impression that a golf course looks like one big wide expanse of grass nicely mown, and that all you have to do is to get your ball from A to B. Unfortunately not.

Don't forget that trees and bushes are allowed to grow; why should they be killed off just because they decide to make your local golf course their home? They are just some of the natural hazards that are there to help make the game that much harder. Don't

forget also that streams exist, and what is more, they have a nasty habit of weaving their way around golf courses.

'Surely there can't be any more hazards?', you're asking yourself. Sorry, but there are, and this time man has put them there deliberately to make your 'simple' task of putting that little white ball into the hole that much more difficult. This time we are facing the problems of bunkers – artificially designed craters in the ground, filled with sand. They are positioned either in front of and/or at the back or side of the green, thus making your approach shot to the green more difficult and calling for extreme accuracy. Some short holes may be virtually

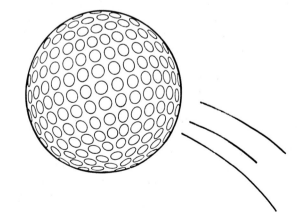

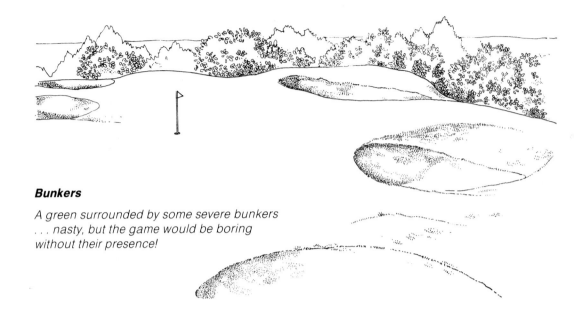

Bunkers

A green surrounded by some severe bunkers
. . . nasty, but the game would be boring
without their presence!

surrounded by bunkers. Bunkers can also be positioned anywhere on the fairway, waiting menacingly for any wayward drive. It is amazing how you can stand on the teeing ground and look down the fairway some 150 yards or so to see this one solitary bunker surrounded by acres of grass, yet your ball always seems to find it! I honestly believe golf course designers have a sadistic streak in them.

Well, if you haven't been put off yet then I think we ought to introduce you to what you will need to play the game with.

The first item of equipment you need is a set of **clubs.** The rules of golf stipulate that fourteen is the maximum number of clubs per set. The rules are also very specific about the design and mouldings of club faces.

A normal set will consist of four wooden clubs, for driving off the tee or playing long shots off the fairway. The inexperienced player, however, will have difficulty using a wood off the fairway. Most woods these days

are in fact not made out of wood at all, but instead have a metal or nylon head coated with a plastic laminate.

For playing fairway shots, whether they be long-distance or delicate chip shots from just off the green, iron clubs graded between nos 1 and 9 are used. The angle of the club face varies as the number of the club gets higher; the higher the number of the club, the greater the angle of the face. Obviously, with a high number club more loft is achieved when playing a shot. Two other irons are often to be found in a set, and are called wedges. One is called the pitching wedge, which is used for playing very lofted or delicate pitch shots to the green. The other is the sand wedge, for playing out of bunkers. (I hope you won't need to use that too often!) Both wedges have very lofted club faces.

The final club, the putter, is, perhaps, the most important of them all. It is on the green that you can gain or lose a lot of strokes during a round, so you want to make sure that you have a putter you are comfortable

Wooden clubs

The putter

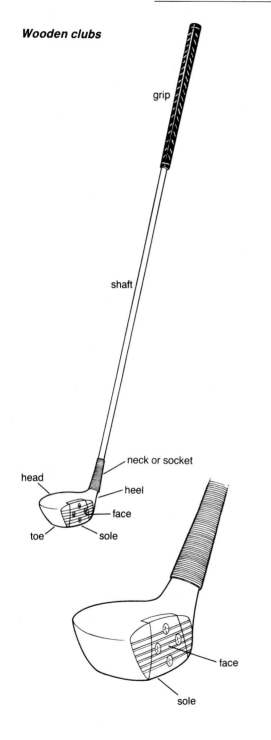

grip

shaft

neck or socket

head

heel

face

toe

sole

face

sole

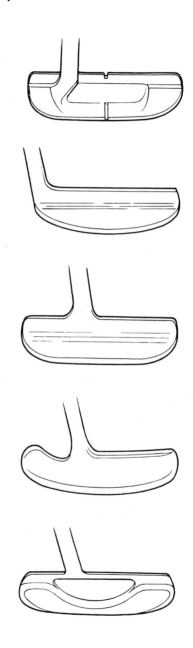

Putters come in a wide variety of shapes and sizes. The above are just a few of those available.

**The club –
a closer look**

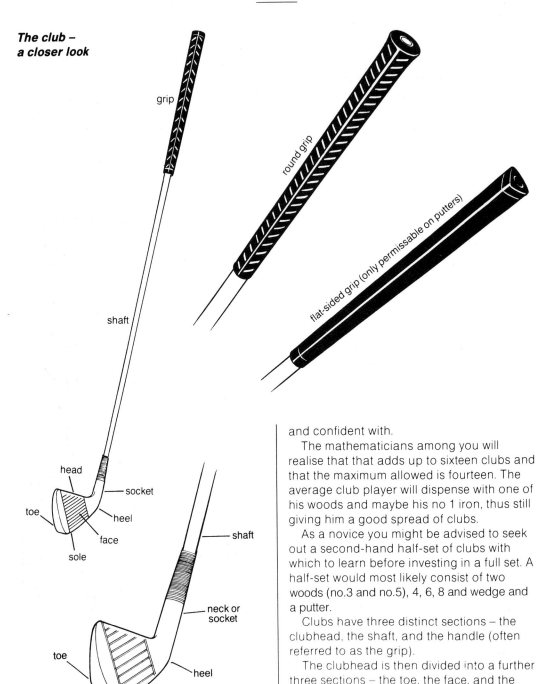

grip

round grip

flat-sided grip (only permissable on putters)

shaft

head

socket

toe

heel

face

sole

shaft

neck or
socket

toe

heel

sole

and confident with.

The mathematicians among you will realise that that adds up to sixteen clubs and that the maximum allowed is fourteen. The average club player will dispense with one of his woods and maybe his no 1 iron, thus still giving him a good spread of clubs.

As a novice you might be advised to seek out a second-hand half-set of clubs with which to learn before investing in a full set. A half-set would most likely consist of two woods (no.3 and no.5), 4, 6, 8 and wedge and a putter.

Clubs have three distinct sections – the clubhead, the shaft, and the handle (often referred to as the grip).

The clubhead is then divided into a further three sections – the toe, the face, and the heel. It is the face that makes contact with the ball. Often you will hear the expression 'he toed it' which means that the toe of the

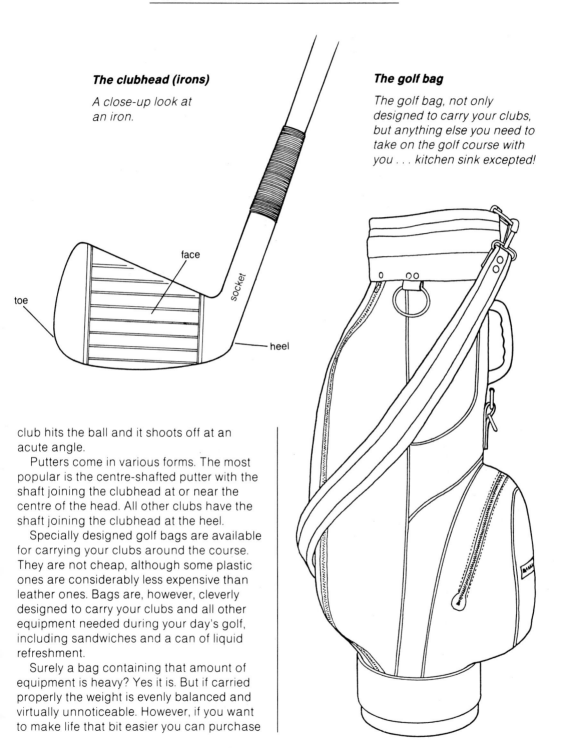

The clubhead (irons)

A close-up look at an iron.

face

socket

toe

heel

The golf bag

The golf bag, not only designed to carry your clubs, but anything else you need to take on the golf course with you . . . kitchen sink excepted!

club hits the ball and it shoots off at an acute angle.

Putters come in various forms. The most popular is the centre-shafted putter with the shaft joining the clubhead at or near the centre of the head. All other clubs have the shaft joining the clubhead at the heel.

Specially designed golf bags are available for carrying your clubs around the course. They are not cheap, although some plastic ones are considerably less expensive than leather ones. Bags are, however, cleverly designed to carry your clubs and all other equipment needed during your day's golf, including sandwiches and a can of liquid refreshment.

Surely a bag containing that amount of equipment is heavy? Yes it is. But if carried properly the weight is evenly balanced and virtually unnoticeable. However, if you want to make life that bit easier you can purchase

GOLF

Playing up the eighteenth hole towards the magnificent clubhouse of the Royal and Ancient Golf Club at St Andrews, the most famous of all golf venues and home of the game.

The golf trolley

If you don't fancy carrying your bag around eighteen holes, a trolley like this can be purchased, or hired, from your club shop.

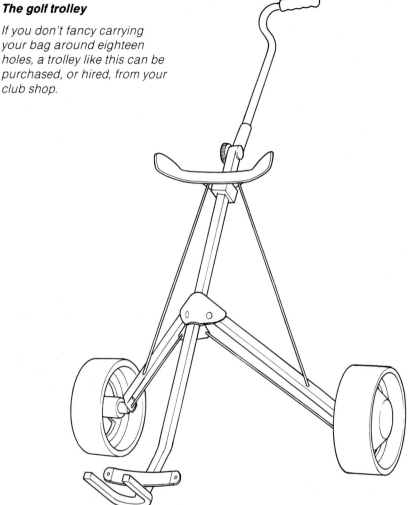

a trolley or hire one from your club shop. All you do is fasten your bag to the trolley and pull it around the course. In the winter many clubs ban the use of trolleys because the wheels damage the fairway in wet conditions. If they don't ban them they will insist on wide-wheeled trolleys only being used. When you buy a trolley, make sure it has interchangeable wheels for summer and winter use.

What about **clothing**? Feeling comfortable is the main criterion when playing golf, but golf clubs are sticklers for tradition and most prohibit the wearing of denims or short trousers (in summer that is!). Slacks and shirt and/or jumper are the common apparel. Many clubs insist on the wearing of a tie in the clubhouse.

Specially-designed golf **shoes** are recommended. They have small spikes on the soles which help you to grip the ground when playing your shot. If you play in ordinary shoes or training shoes in wet weather your feet will slide as you twist to play your shot. The result . . . the club won't be where it should be when it makes contact with the ball. Therefore, a pair of golf shoes is a wise investment.

A **glove** also makes the playing of shots that much easier. Made of leather, only one is worn, if you are right-handed you wear it on your left hand and vice versa if you are left-handed. The glove enhances your grip of the club. Many players prefer to take their glove off when putting.

For those rainy days, and in Britain there are plenty of them, you need protection from the elements, and a good set of **waterproofs** is recommended. They are made of very lightweight material these days and fold up to fit easily into your bag. Because they are so light, they are less restrictive than they used to be. And of course for those rainy days an **umbrella** is also a must. There is nothing worse than getting wet whilst walking between shots. Remember, never put your umbrella up in a storm as it may be struck by lightning. In any case, you should get off the course if thunder and lightning start. Whatever you do, don't shelter under a tree – you might regret it.

The glove

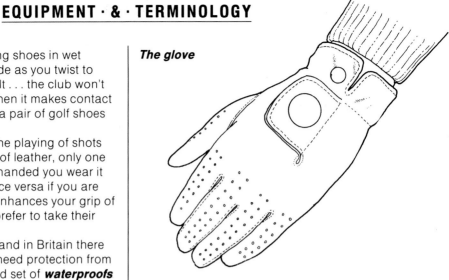

A vital part of your golfing equipment . . . the glove.

Right, that's the clubs, bag, trolley and clothing. Finally the **ball** – that little menace which poses all the problems on a golf course.

We have seen earlier how the golf ball has developed over the years. The current ball is round, normally white, and the outer casing is impregnated with a series of dimples to improve its aerodynamics. For years the

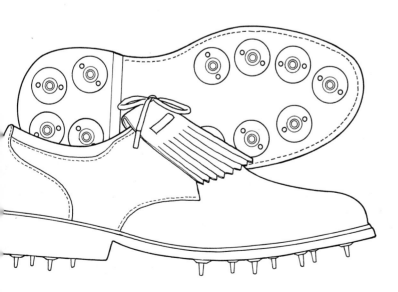

Golf shoes

A typical pair of golf shoes, with removable spikes.

GOLF

The ball

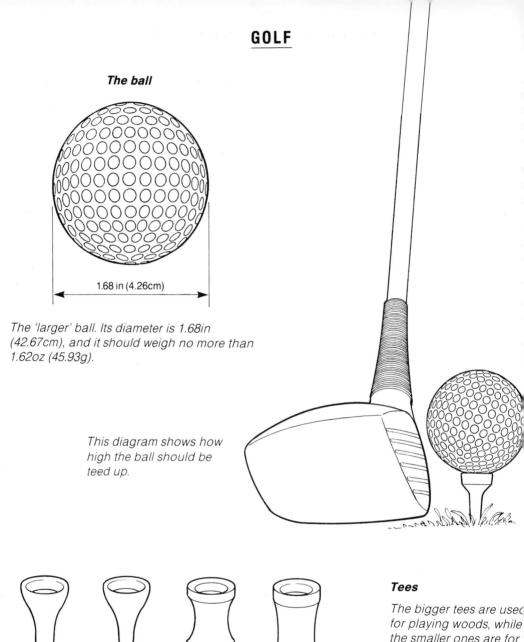

1.68 in (4.26cm)

The 'larger' ball. Its diameter is 1.68in (42.67cm), and it should weigh no more than 1.62oz (45.93g).

This diagram shows how high the ball should be teed up.

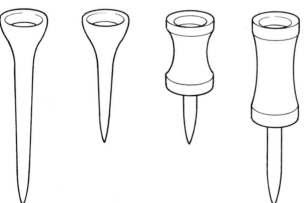

Tees

The bigger tees are used for playing woods, while the smaller ones are for irons. The tees on the right are depressed into the ground to the lip, thus marking the ideal height from which the ball should be played.

Americans used a larger ball than the British, but since the 1974 Open the larger ball has been the accepted ball and is now the one commonly used in Britain. The current dimensions of the larger ball are 1·68in (42·67mm) diameter and with a weight not exceeding 1·62oz (45·93g). It is useful to carry a piece of towelling in your bag to clean your ball (and clubheads) with.

In order to make the driving of the first ball at each hole that much easier, a plastic or wooden **tee** is permitted. About 2in (5cm) in length it is placed in the ground and the ball placed on top of it at the desired height. Tees can only be used on the teeing ground and not on the fairway, although, if local rules permit, balls on the fairway may be 'teed up' (on a clump of grass, leaves, etc, but not with a tee) so as not to cause damage to the fairway.

A **scorecard** and pencil are needed to keep a note of your own and your opponent's score. All clubs provide a scorecard for your use at the commencement of each round. It is your responsibility to keep a note of your opponent's score, and he should do the same for you. At the end of a round, if you are playing in a competition or submitting your score to the club for consideration for a handicap, the card must be signed by both players.

And finally, you always need to carry plenty of money on you. Should you ever be lucky enough to achieve it, a hole-in-one will cost you a few pounds in drinks in the club-house afterwards! Golf's most sociable tradition is that you should buy everyone a drink after scoring a hole-in-one, but fortunately it does not happen very often!

The scorecard

Player A_____H'cap_____

Player B_____H'cap_____

Date_____

Event_____

Marks Score	Hole	Yards	Metres	Par	Stroke Index	Score A	B	Won X Lost – H'ld. O
	1	328	300	4	15			
	2	106	97	3	17			
	3	425	388	4	5			
	4	474	433	4	1			
	5	315	288	4	13			
	6	190	174	3	9			
	7	485	443	5	7			
	8	360	329	4	11			
	9	365	334	4	3			
		3048	2786	35	OUT			

Marks Score	Hole	Yards	Metres	Par	Stroke Index	Score A	B	Won X Lost – H'ld. O
	10	190	174	3	12			
	11	346	316	4	10			
	12	524	479	5	4			
	13	179	164	3	14			
	14	393	359	4	8			
	15	327	299	4	16			
	16	430	393	4	2			
	17	291	266	4	18			
	18	403	368	4	6			
		3083	2818	35	HOME			
Out		3048	2786	35	—			
Total		6131	5604	70	—			
H'cap		—	—	—	—			
Nett		—	—	—	—			

Competitors Sig._____

Markers Sig._____

A typical scorecard, showing the length of each hole in yards and metres, and the stroke index of each. The stroke index column tells the player the order in which strokes are received or given over the 18 holes. The front of the card indicates local rules, out of bound areas and the positions of water hazards.

TERMINOLOGY

The next stage is to explain the rules of golf and show you how to play the game. First, however, in order to make the rest of the book that much easier, I think you ought to familiarize yourself with some of the most common golfing terms:

Ace   Another name for a hole-in-one, particularly used in America.

Address   A player takes up his address when he adopts his normal stance and grounds the clubhead behind the ball. You are not allowed to ground the clubhead in a bunker or hazard.

Albatross   The playing of a hole in three strokes under the regulated par. A hole-in-one at a par-4 would be an albatross. A par-5 hole completed in two shots would also be an albatross.

Approach shot   Any shot made towards the green from anywhere other than the tee is an approach shot.

Apron   The area around the perimeter of the green is known as the apron. It is cut shorter than the fairway but not as short as the green.

Back door putt   A putt that rolls around the hole and enters it from the back is known as a back door, or tradesman's entrance, putt.

Back nine   The last nine holes of a round are the back nine. They are also called the second nine, or inward half.

Backswing   The backswing is the movement of the clubhead away from the ball to a point where the clubhead, when at the back of your head, starts its downward swing towards the ball. The backswing is one of the most important movements in the golf swing. It should not be rushed, and the action of taking the clubhead away from the ball should be smooth and fluent.

Best ball   A match when one player competes against two or three others is known as a best ball. The score of the

The address

The address is taken up when you have adopted your normal stance and have grounded the club behind the ball.

The backswing

This diagram shows the club drawn back to the top of the backswing. Note now the head has hardly moved and how the player's eyes are firmly fixed on the ball.

individual player is matched against the best score of the other players. It is suitable for both match-play and stroke-play.

Better ball   It can only be used in a match containing four players. The score of the lowest scoring player on each team counts at each hole. Again it is suitable for both match-play and stroke-play.

Birdie   Any hole played out in one stroke under the regulated par score is a birdie. A par-4 hole played in three shots is an example and is described as a 'birdie 3'.

Bogey   In Britain, strictly-speaking the word 'bogey' means the number of strokes in which a player is expected to complete a hole, or a complete round. However, the more common use of the word is the American version, which describes a hole that has been played in one stroke over the allotted par figure. A par 4 played in five shots would be described as a 'bogey 5'.

Caddie   The person who carries a golfer's clubs and generally assists with his playing of the round is a caddie. Caddies were first used in the early seventeenth century.

Carry   The carry is a term used to describe the distance a golf ball travels from the moment it is hit to the point where it first touches the ground.

Casual water   Casual water is a temporary accumulation of water on the course. If your ball lands in casual water you may remove it and drop it without penalty. Streams, lakes and ponds are not described as casual water, but snow and ice are.

Chip   A chip shot is played as an approach shot to the green.

Closed stance   A 'closed' stance is taken up by moving your left foot slightly forward of the line of target. (See Technique section for further explanation).

Cut (1)   Another word for a slice.

Cut (2)   The point where the field in large competitions is reduced. Normally made after the first thirty-six holes of a seventy-two-hole competition and again after the next eighteen holes.

Divot   A piece of turf taken out of the ground by the clubhead after making contact with the ball. Good players will often deliberately take a divot with their shot in order to impart backspin on the ball and stop it more quickly.

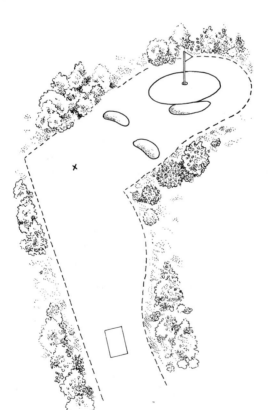

The dogleg

This is a dogleg to the right. The best way to play it is to drive down the fairway to position 'x', and then play your second shot to the green.

Draw

Intentional 'bending' of the ball to the left is known as 'draw'.

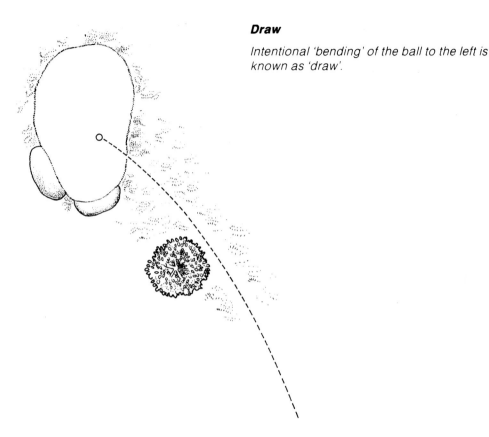

Dogleg   Any hole that has the green situated at an angle from the fairway, and often hidden from the tee, is a dogleg.

Dormie   In match-play a player is said to be dormie if he cannot lose. In other words, if he is winning by two holes and there are only two holes left to play then he is 'dormie 2'. If, however, extra holes are required to find a winner, a player cannot therefore be said to be dormie.

Double bogey   A hole played in two over the allotted par score is a double bogey. A par-4 hole played in six shots would be a 'double bogey 6'.

Double eagle   The American term for an albatross.

Draw   Playing a controlled shot with the ball travelling to the right before coming in left towards its intended target.

Driver   The most powerful club in your bag. Commonly known as the no.1 wood. As a beginner you should get used to your other woods before trying the driver.

Drop   There may be times when it is impossible to play your ball. The rules will tell you in which circumstances you can pick up and drop your ball without incurring a penalty or whether you must incur one. When dropping a ball it must be from shoulder height and at arms length and the ball must land no nearer the hole.

Eagle   A hole played in two strokes under

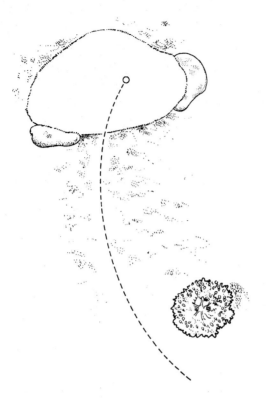

Fade

The opposite of 'draw', the 'fade' is a deliberate shot that causes the ball to 'bend' to the right.

the par score for the hole is an eagle. A par-4 played in two strokes is an 'eagle 2'.

Etiquette   Golf, perhaps more than any other sport, has a code of etiquette laws which should be observed at all times. For further details see page 44.

Extra holes   If a winner of a major competition has still to be found after the completion of all the rounds, then extra holes will be played. The number will depend upon the rules of the competition. In match-play events it will be on a sudden-death basis until one player wins a hole. In stroke-play events it may be over eighteen more holes. If extra holes are required they do not necessarily start again at the first tee. It can be from any tee as agreed. In televised events the extra holes are generally those which can easily be covered by cameras. At club level, if the final scores are level, a winner is normally found by a card 'play-off'. This could mean, for example, that the player with the lowest score over the first nine holes is proclaimed the winner.

Fade   The opposite to draw; it is a controlled shot in which the ball starts out to the left before turning right into its intended target.

Flight   The flight of the ball is determined

Payne Stewart demonstrates the delicate touch needed to play accurate shots from greenside bunkers.

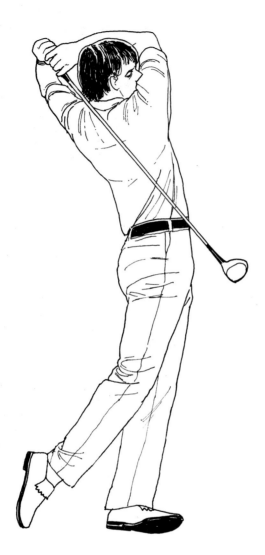

Follow-through

A perfect example of the follow-through.

by the loft of the club used for the shot. The flight is the path the ball takes as it travels through the air. Obviously, the flight of the ball is seriously affected if you fail to make proper contact.

Follow-through   The follow-through is vital in golf, just as it is to many other sports. It is the completion of the swing *after* the club has made contact with the ball.

Fore   A shout used by golfers to warn another player that a ball is heading in his direction. Basically you are telling the other player to get out of the way before the ball hits him.

Four ball   A four ball is a match involving four players. The outcome can be resolved in varying ways. It can be either stroke- or match-play and either the better ball of each

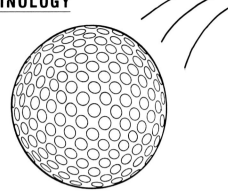

pair at every hole shall count, or the aggregate scores of the two players on each team shall count if stroke-play.

Foursomes   Again played by two per side but this time both players of one side take it in turns to hit the same ball. They must, however, take it in turns to drive.

Front nine   The first nine holes of a round are the front nine. Also known as the first nine or the outward nine.

Gimmie   A term used in match-play when a ball is so close to the hole that it is virtually impossible to miss it and it is 'given' by the opposing player or team.

Green fee   The green fee is the amount of money you have to pay to play a round of golf as a visitor to a private club or at a municipal club.

Grip   The grip is the way a player holds the club. (This is explained in greater detail in the Technique section). The handle of the club is also referred to as the grip.

Gross score   Your gross score is the number of strokes you take to complete a hole, or a round. Your handicap is deducted to give you your net score.

Grounding the club   When the clubhead is placed on the ground behind the ball it is said to be grounded. It must **not** be grounded in the bunkers or hazards.

Ground under repair   From time to time it is necessary to repair part of the golf course. That area is deemed to be ground under repair and any ball landing in it must be removed, without penalty.

Half   A match or hole is halved if both players' (or teams') scores are level at the end of the match or hole and both are credited with a half.

Handicap   The attraction of golf is that it allows players of different standards to compete against each other on equal terms, thanks to the handicap system. It is one of the few games in the world where 'all men are equal' and, theoretically, both men stand an equal chance of winning. The handicap system was introduced in Great Britain in 1926. It is explained fully in the 'Game Guide' on page 47.

Hazards   While you may think that a hazard is any obstruction doing its level best to stop you reaching your goal, putting the ball in the hole, the rules of golf define a hazard as: 'Any bunker or water hazard'. Trees, telegraph poles etc, are not termed hazards according to the rules . . . but believe me, get stuck behind one and it is a hazard all right.

Holing out   The final act, whether in elation or despair, of putting the ball into the hole.

Hole-in-one   Hitting the ball into the hole direct from the tee is a hole-in-one (called an ace in America). It is very rare for a hole-in-one to be obtained at a hole other than a par-3.

Honour   The person who drives first at each hole is said to 'have the honour'. At the first tee this is mutually agreed, or decided by the toss of a coin. Thereafter the person winning the hole goes first.

GOLF

Lateral water hazard

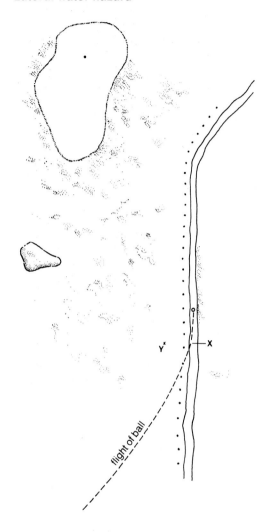

flight of ball

A lateral water hazard runs parallel to the fairway and is marked with red posts. If a ball enters a lateral water hazard it can be played where it lies, if possible, or may be dropped from a point (y) two club-lengths away from the point where it crossed the edge of the hazard (x) . . . but not nearer the hole.

Hook A shot that bends to the left of its intended target is a hook, when played by a right-handed golfer. Vice versa for the left-handed.

In play A ball is in play from the moment it is struck until the moment it is holed out. If it goes out of bounds or is lifted or lost, it is no longer in play.

Inward half The last nine holes of a round are the inward half. Also known as the second half or back nine.

Lateral water hazard A lateral water hazard is a water hazard that runs parallel to the fairway and should be marked with red marker posts or lines.

Lie The position of the ball when it comes to rest is its lie. It must be played from that point unless impossible or the rules state otherwise.

Lip The edge of the hole is the lip. Quite often the ball will hang on the lip without dropping in. Then it is called by another name, but that is unprintable . . !

Local rules While all golf clubs in Britain play to the same basic rules, your club may have a few rules peculiar to itself. These are called local rules. There is a course in Australia that forms part of a local landing strip. Local rules state that 'Aircraft have the right of way at all times'!

Loft Loft is the amount of height obtained on a ball after playing it. It also refers to the angle of the club face.

Loose impediments Natural objects such as twigs, leaves and branches are loose impediments, provided they are not growing. Sand and loose soil are loose impediments, but only on the putting green. Loose impediments may be removed if they are hindering your stroke. Natural objects are not movable in a hazard.

Lost ball Self explanatory . . . the rules however, allow you five minutes to find a lost ball. If after that time it is still not found, the shot must be played again from a spot near to where it was last played, and under a penalty of one stroke.

Match A contest between either two players, or two sides, is described as a match.

Match-play A contest in which the players or teams attempt to win more holes than their opponent(s). Aggregate scores at the end of the round are irrelevant and the total number of holes won or lost counts. If a player is leading by three holes and only two are remaining, he cannot lose and is said to be the winner '3 & 2'. If the scores are all square going to the last hole and one player wins it he is said to have won by '1 hole'. If a player leads by three with three holes remaining ('dormie 3' – remember?) and then wins the next hole, he is four holes up with two to play and that is where the match ends with him winning '4 & 2'.

Medal round Another name for stroke-play competition.

Nap Like a snooker table a golf green has a nap and it runs in the direction it was cut. A ball hit with the nap of the green will travel faster than one hit against it.

Net score Your score at the end of the round *after* deducting your handicap. If you are a 24-handicap player and complete a round in 97 then your net score is 73.

Nineteenth hole The common expression for the clubhouse bar!

Open stance The opposite to a closed stance. It is when, after adopting your normal stance, you pull your left foot back from the intended line of flight. (See Technique section for further explanation).

Out of bounds Specifically laid down areas on golf courses are out of bounds. The perimeter fence or wall of any course normally signifies an out of bounds area but often artificial boundaries are created to prevent wayward shots. Any ball that goes out of bounds must be replayed from a spot near to where the ball was last played, and under a one-stroke penalty. The out of bounds lines are defined by white posts.

Outward nine The first nine holes of a round are known as the outward nine. Also known as the first nine or front nine.

Par The par of a hole is the number of shots a good golfer would be expected to take to complete the hole. The par of each hole is decided by its length alone and not by its difficulty. The following lengths are used to define the par of a hole in Britain:
  Par-3: Under 251yd (229m).
  Par-4: 251yd (229m) to 475yd (434m).
  Par-5: 476yd (435m) and over.

Penalty stroke A penalty stroke is added to your score if you are in breach of any rule that incurs a penalty.

Pin high

*Both these balls are said to be
'pin high', because they have
landed level with the pin.*

Pin high   If a ball lands on the green
adjacent to the flag, but to the right or left of
it, it is said to be pin high.

Pitch   A shot played, normally with a
wedge, when close to the green.

Pitch and run   A pitch, but played with no
backspin so that the ball will continue
running forward when it hits the green.

Pitch mark   If a ball is played with a lofted
club onto the green it will leave an
indentation, known as a pitch mark. You
should always repair such a mark, with
either a tee or special fork, so as not to leave
the pitch mark and thus hinder other
players' putting.

Plugged ball   A ball is plugged if it remains
in its own pitch mark after hitting the green,
bunker or fairway. Unless local rules permit
otherwise, the ball must be played from
where it comes to rest. Plugged balls occur
more often in wet conditions.

Preferred lie   In the winter months, so as
not to damage the fairway, most clubs
introduce the 'preferred lies' rule, which
permits you to move your ball to a position
where you are less likely to take a divot or
damage the fairway.

Putting   The art of hitting the ball on the
green with the putter is known as putting.

Round   A round of golf normally consists of
eighteen holes which must be played in the
correct numerical sequence.

Run   After a ball finishes bouncing it will
run on for a while before coming to rest. This
is known as the run of the ball.

Scratch   A very good golfer who does not
need a handicap is a scratch golfer.

Semi-rough   The area between the fairway
and rough is called the semi-rough. It is not
as long as the rough, but longer than the
fairway.

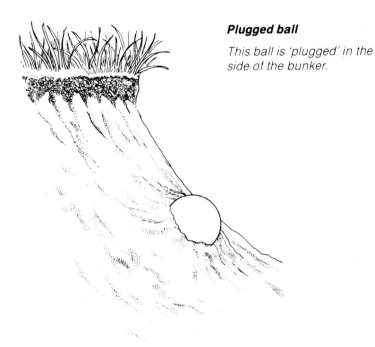

Plugged ball

This ball is 'plugged' in the side of the bunker.

Slice   A ball that bends sharply to the right of its intended target is said to be sliced. This assumes it was played by a right-handed player. It is vice versa for the left-hander.

Stableford   A Stableford is a type of competition (named after its inventor, Dr Frank Stableford). Points are awarded according to how many strokes under or over par you take to complete a hole. The scoring is as follows:

    Par + 2 or more: 0 pts
    Par + 1: 1 pt
    Par: 2 pts
    Par − 1: 3pts
    Par − 2: 4 pts
    Par − 3: 5 pts

The number of points gained at each hole is added together to give an aggregate score.

Stance   The position taken up by a player as he addresses the ball. The stance varies according to the needs of the shot. (See the Technique section for further explanation.)

Stroke   A forward movement with the club with the intention of hitting the ball is a stroke and counts as one shot played. Even if it misses the ball, and the intention **was** to hit it, the stroke counts as one shot. This is commonly known as an 'air shot'.

Stroke index   When you get a scorecard, you will see alongside each hole number the length and par of that hole. Each will be graded between 1 and 18. All holes are graded according to their difficulty (the hardest is stroke index number 1).

Stroke play   Also known as medal play, a player's net score is taken into consideration and the one with the lowest score is the winner of any match or competition.

Sudden-death play-off   If a winner of a competition has to be found and a pre-determined number of extra holes are not being played, the competition will be decided by a sudden-death play-off. The first person to win a hole is deemed the winner.

GOLF

Swing   The swing is the continuous movement of the clubhead from the moment it leaves its address position, to the top of its backswing, down to when it hits the ball, and on into the follow-through.

Takeaway   The first movement of the club from its address position as it starts its backswing is the takeaway.

Tee   The small wooden or plastic peg used for teeing up the ball on the teeing ground.

Texas wedge   A shot played off the putting surface with the putter (fully permissible) was christened a Texas wedge by the Americans.

Three ball   A match involving three players who each use their own ball.

Threesome   A match involving three players, but two play against one. The twosome play alternate shots at the same ball.

Topped   A ball is 'topped' if the clubhead makes contact with the top half of the ball as opposed to hitting it cleanly in the bottom half or centre.

Trap   The American name for a bunker.

Water hazards   The rules of golf define a water hazard as: any sea, lake, pond, river, ditch, surface drainage ditch or other open water course (whether or not containing water) and anything of a similar nature. Water hazards should be marked by yellow lines or stakes.

Laura Davies has achieved international success and adds to the interest in the ladies' events wherever she plays.

THE GAME – A GUIDE

A s I have said already, golf is basically a simple game. It is a matter of hitting the ball from the teeing area down the fairway, onto the green and into the hole. What could be more simple? However, even the best players cannot do that all the time, and they must be ready for the unexpected. For you, the club player, the unexpected will happen more often than not! Consequently, the rules of golf are complex and allow for every possible eventuality. For example, what happens if a rabbit runs across the fairway and takes off with your ball? These questions are all dealt with in the rules.

Before we go into any intricacies, we should start off with the etiquette rules of golf. These will then give you an insight into what you can and cannot do. They have nothing to do with how well you play the game, but have an important bearing on how you should conduct yourself when playing.

Golf's etiquette rules

● The player who has the honour of playing first should be allowed to tee his ball before any other player.
● No player or caddie should talk or stand near to a player when he is about to play, or stand directly behind a hole when he is putting.

● There is nothing worse than hanging around behind a slow party of players in front of you, so . . . don't dawdle, get on with your game.
● It is also infuriating waiting behind a match that is taking time to find a lost ball. If it is obvious you are going to spend time looking for a ball then call the match behind you to 'play through'.
● Once you have completed a hole, leave the green immediately; don't stand there analysing your shots, and don't forget to replace the flagstick.
● Golf is a dangerous game . . . so don't play your next shot if players in front of you are still within your hitting range.
● In terms of preference, two-ball matches have preference over three- and four-ball matches. People playing on their own have no standing on the golf course and cannot expect to be called through.
● The golf course is a sacred area and must be treated with the utmost respect. Replace all divots, as we have already said. Use waste bins for any discarded items, and after playing out of a bunker, make sure you smooth over your footprints. *You* wouldn't like it if your ball had landed in the footprint left by somebody ahead of you would you? Look after the green as well by repairing any damage your spikes might have caused or if your ball has created a plug mark.

● Never take your trolley or golf bag onto the green, and if you put the flagstick onto the green, don't throw it down – place it gently.

Etiquette is golf's number one rule. Abide by the code and, while it may not improve your game, it will make you welcome on any golf course.

Now for the rules . . .
There are thirty-four rules of golf. A lot of them are best explained in the Rules Clinic which appears on pages 48–53. However, the main rules will be covered in this section.

A game

A game consists of playing the ball from the teeing position into each hole by a stroke or succession of strokes. You are not allowed to move the ball in any manner other than with the club, unless the rules otherwise stipulate (i.e. to move the ball in order to drop it). A game normally consists of one complete round of eighteen holes, unless the length of course or rules of the competition dictate otherwise.

Types of play

There are two principal types of play, **match-play** and **stroke-play**. In match-play the match is decided by the number of holes won or lost. At the end of each hole the player with the lowest score, after his handicap has been deducted, is the winner. If both players have the same score, the hole is halved. Scoring is not done by adding each player's holes won together, but by quoting the difference between player A and player B. For example, if after seven holes you had won three, lost one and halved three, then you would be '2-Up' with eleven to play (assuming you were playing over eighteen holes).

Because your actual score on the hole doesn't matter, provided you complete it in fewer strokes than your opponent, either player may concede a hole at any given time. If, for example, you have driven straight on to the green and your opponent has hit two balls out of bounds, he would be playing his fifth shot off the tee. As you are already on the green, it is hardly worth his while carrying on and he would most likely pick the ball up and concede the hole.

Stroke-play is different. Your score at each hole is important, and it is your aggregate score at the end of the pre-determined number of holes that determines the winner. You must hole out on every green and 'gimmies' are not allowed in stroke-play.

The clubs

All clubs must conform to the specifications laid down by the Royal and Ancient, and you must not carry more than fourteen clubs in your bag at any one time. Clubs must be complete and in one unit and not be adjustable in any way, except in weight. Any

Grooves

The rules stipulate the design and size of grooves on club faces.

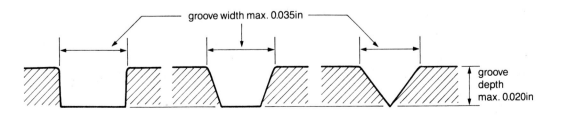

groove width max. 0.035in

groove depth max. 0.020in

club damaged during the normal course of play must remain in that state until the end of the round. Remember Ben Crenshaw damaging his putter in a temper during the 1987 Ryder Cup . . . he ended up putting with all sorts of different clubs!

The ball

A standard ball as laid down in the rules shall be used. If a ball becomes unfit for play it can be picked up and examined, but advance notice must be given to your opponent(s) that you are taking this action. If it is visibly cut, cracked or out of shape it can be replaced. A ball cannot be cleaned to see if it is damaged.

Order of play

The honour to play first is decided before the start of the match. Honour to start the next and subsequent holes falls upon the person winning the last hole. If a hole is halved then the person who had the honour at the previous hole retains it. In stroke-play, the player with the lowest score at each hole plays first at the next hole, and players follow in ascending order depending upon their score.

Once all balls have been played from the teeing ground the player whose ball is furthest from the hole shall play first. If a player plays out of turn in match-play he can

be called upon immediately to abandon that shot and play another shot when it is his turn, and from the same spot, but without penalty. In stroke-play no penalty is incurred for playing out of turn and the ball is played as it lies.

It may be necessary to play a provisional ball from the tee in case your first one cannot be found. If you have to play a 'provisional' it should be done after all the other players have teed off.

Playing the ball

The ball, once played from the tee, must be played as it lies (unless local rules allow for its movement, i.e. preferred lies etc.). You must not make any attempt with your body, club, or any other article to improve the lie of the ball. If the ball is unplayable, however, it has to be moved and dropped in accordance with the rules, either under penalty or otherwise. If your ball rests under leaves or broken branches they can be removed without penalty, provided you do not move your ball at the same time. But anything which is not a loose impediment cannot be removed.

On the green

Once your ball is on the putting green you must not interfere with the line of putt, and furthermore must not impede or interfere with your opponent's line of putt. You may remove any pieces of sand, soil or other loose impediments in your line of putt by either picking them up or brushing them aside. Naturally, if there is a plug mark previously unrepaired in your line of putt you can repair it.

You can lift your ball off the putting surface and clean it, but it must be returned to the spot where it lay. Most club shops sell small circular plastic markers for marking the position of your ball before you remove it from the putting surface.

Whatever you do, you must not practise a

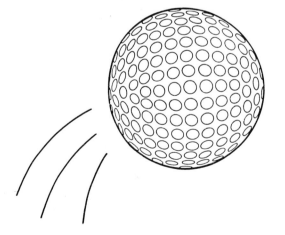

putt with another ball, or roll a ball on the putting surface to see how it is running.

Once on the green you may have the flag left in the hole and attended by another player or caddie, or taken out of the hole. But you must indicate your preference before you take your putt. The attendant must remove the flag before the ball hits it.

If you are playing from just off the green you can ask for the flag to be taken out, attended, or even left. If your ball rests against the flag in this case, you can ask another player or caddie to remove it and if the ball drops in the hole it is deemed to be holed.

That about takes care of the basics of the game, but as we said earlier there is a lot more to it than that. I still haven't told you what happens when that rabbit runs off with your ball. Hopefully the next chapter will clear up some of the finer points of the game. Before we do that I think we ought to outline the handicap system and show how it works.

Handicapping

A player's handicap is basically the average number of strokes that he takes to go round the golf course over the Standard Scratch Score, or normal par for the course, under usual stroke-play conditions. The maximum handicap for men is 28 strokes and for women 36. Obviously, the more ability a player has, the lower his handicap will be. For example, a very able player with a handicap of 5 should, theoretically at least, complete every round of golf he plays within only five strokes of the par for the course, under normal stroke-play conditions. A player of less ability, with a handicap of, say, 24, has more strokes above par allowed to him, to compensate for his lesser skill. If a player with a handicap of 5 plays one with a handicap of 24, the former effectively 'gives' the latter nineteen strokes over the round, i.e. the difference between 5 and 24.

The responsibility of fixing a player's handicap rests with his club. He must be an amateur player and a member of a club affiliated to the Council of National Golf Unions. After a player has submitted three scorecards, the handicap committee will fix a handicap according to an average of the number of strokes over par which the player made during each of his three rounds. Handicaps fall into four categories, as follows:

Handicap	Category
5 or less	1
6–12	2
13–20	3
21–28	4

In women's golf, the handicaps as laid down by the Ladies Golf Union are different, and are as follows:

Handicap	Category
3 or less	A
4–6	B
7–18	C
19–29	D
30–36	E

Right, on to some more rules. . .

RULES CLINIC

Can I apply any substance or material to my clubhead?

No. You must not apply any foreign material to any of your clubs, nor must you interfere with their design. Penalty is disqualification from a tournament.

How am I penalized if I have more than fourteen clubs in my bag?

At the end of the hole when it was discovered you had too many clubs you would be penalized as follows:
In match-play you are penalized by deducting one hole for each hole at which the breach of the rules occurred, subject to a maximum deduction of two holes per round. In stroke-play the penalty is two strokes at each hole at which any breach occurred, subject to a maximum of four strokes per round.

So, if I have fifteen clubs in my bag do I have to throw one away?

Of course not. But you must declare one club 'out of play' and you must not use it. If you do, you are liable to disqualification.

If a ball breaks in two, or shatters after I've played my shot what happens?

The stroke can be played again, and without any penalty . . . with a replacement ball of course!

I understand how the handicap works in stroke-play – it is just deducted from my score to provide a net score. But how does it work in match-play?

The handicap allowance is $\frac{3}{4}$ the difference between the two players' handicaps. If you played off 16 and your opponent off 12, the difference is 4. You would therefore be entitled to strokes at the first three holes on the stroke index. In a foursome match-play game the handicaps of both players per side are added together. The allowance is then $\frac{3}{8}$ the difference between the highest and lowest aggregate.

What about fractions when working out the handicap in match-play? How do they work out?

Anything under $\frac{1}{2}$ is ignored, and anything over $\frac{1}{2}$ is rounded up to the nearest whole number. For example $\frac{3}{4}$ of 21 is $15\frac{3}{4}$. This would be rounded up to 16. If your handicap, however, was 15, then it would work out at $11\frac{1}{4}$ which would be 11 for match-play purposes.

What about Stableford competitions. How does the handicap work then?

As in match-play, except that $\frac{7}{8}$ of your handicap is used to calculate your allowance.

If I'm playing in a competition, can I have a practice round before the competition starts?

No. You may, of course, practise on the specially provided practice ground and putting areas, but not on the course itself. Do so and you could be disqualified.

What happens if my ball falls off the tee or is knocked off while I'm lining up my shot?

It can be replaced without penalty. It is only counted if you play a completed stroke at it.

Can a caddie stand over a player with an umbrella to protect him from the rain in dreadful conditions?

Yes, but *not* while he is playing a stroke. It is a two-shot penalty if stroke-play, or loss of the hole if match-play.

I know the answer will be no, but can I hit a moving ball?

Why did you bother asking then? The answer *is* no, and if you do you will be penalized two strokes in stroke-play, or the loss of the hole if match-play.

I'm on the tee, have addressed my ball and started my swing. At the last minute I don't feel comfortable and want to abort the swing, but the clubhead touches the ball and knocks it off the tee just a couple of inches. Can I re-take the shot?

You never used to be able to, but from 1 January 1988 the rules were changed and now say that if the downswing is checked it is not deemed to be a stroke. Therefore you can replace your ball.

Who plays, and in what order if there are four of us playing?

Let's say you are playing stroke-play. The following example should clarify it. Player A has the honour at the first hole . . . right, this is how it works from then on.

Hole	Scores					Order of play at next hole			
	A	B	C	D					
1	5	5	4	5		C	A	B	D
2	5	4	4	4		C	B	D	A
3	5	5	5	5		C	B	D	A
4	3	4	4	4		A	C	B	D
5	7	6	5	4		D	C	B	A

. . . and so on.

GOLF

If a ball has to be dropped how does one go about it?

The spot where the ball lay has to be marked. The ball must then be dropped by the player himself by holding the ball at shoulder height and arm's length and dropping it.

Where should a ball be dropped?

As near to its original position as possible but not nearer the hole (except where a rule permits it to be dropped elsewhere). If a ball has to be dropped in a hazard (bunker, etc.) then it must land in the hazard after being dropped.

If a dropped ball rolls out of bounds am I penalized further?

No. If it does you can re-drop without penalty. Likewise, if it rolls out of a hazard when it should be in it, or into one when it shouldn't be in it. If the dropped ball rolls on to the putting green it can also be re-dropped, and if it rolls to the spot from where relief was originally gained, a re-drop is allowed without penalty. Also, if the ball comes to rest more than two club lengths from where it first struck the ground after the drop, or comes to rest nearer the hole than permitted, then the ball must be dropped again. If, after a re-drop it still rolls to one of the positions outlined above it will then be *placed* at a point near to where it first hit the ground on the re-drop.

If I'm on the putting green and a puddle is in my line of putt do I have to play the shot from where the ball is or can I move it?

You can play it if you want, but you would not be wise to do so. You can move your ball, without penalty, to the first available space on the green giving you relief from the casual water, but without being nearer to the hole. You do not drop your ball when re-positioning it, but place it by hand in its new position.

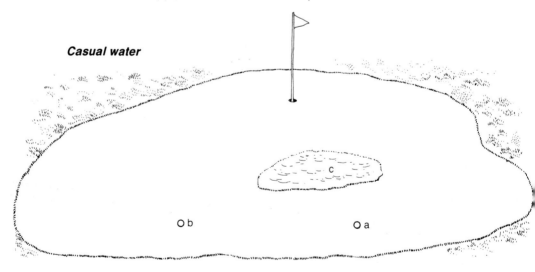

Casual water

If your ball is in position (a) you can putt through the casual water (c), but this is not advised. Alternatively, you can move your ball the first available space for relief to (b), but it must not be nearer the hole than at position (a).

What happens if my ball lands on the wrong putting green, do I have to play from where it lies?

No, you most pick up your ball and drop it, without penalty. The point where you drop it must be off the green but not nearer the hole you are playing towards, and must not be in a hazard. It is dropped in the normal manner and it must be one club's length from the point determined.

What happens if my ball goes into a water hazard?

You can play it from where it lies! Alternatively you can play another shot from where you last played, but under a one-stroke penalty. Or you can drop the ball, under a one-stroke penalty, behind the water hazard, but keeping the point where the ball crossed the hazard between yourself and the hole. You can drop the ball as far behind the hazard as you wish.

Surely I couldn't drop a ball behind a lateral water hazard, because you said in the definitions that a lateral water hazard runs parallel to the fairway. If I dropped the ball behind it I'd still be in the water . . . ?

Well spotted . . . In such a case you would drop the ball on the fairway-side of the hazard two club lengths away from where the ball entered the hazard, or at any point on the other side of the hazard, but in both cases not nearer the hole, and in both cases under a one-stroke penalty.

What happens if my ball is lost or goes out of bounds?

If the ball is lost outside a water hazard, or goes out of bounds then you play another shot from where you last played the ball under a one-stroke penalty.

Dropping from a water hazard

If your ball goes into a water hazard (not a lateral water hazard), you can either play it (if playable) or drop it. You can drop anywhere behind the hazard, but the point where the ball entered it (x), must be directly between you and the hole. In this case, anywhere along the dotted line x – y.

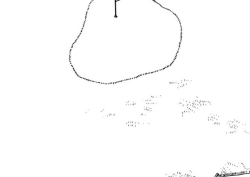

Please explain the rule about playing a provisional ball?

If, after playing a shot it seems apparent your ball is not likely to be found, or appears to have gone out of bounds, you can advise your playing partner of your intention to play another ball – a provisional ball. You play it in the normal way (and hopefully you don't lose that one as well!). If your first ball is not found then you play your next shot from where the provisional ball came to rest but add one penalty stroke to your score. However, if your original ball is found, the provisional ball is picked up and you carry on playing with the original ball and without any penalty.

If my ball comes to rest adjacent to my opponent's on the fairway can one of the balls be moved?

Yes, and without penalty. It must be replaced as soon as the other player has taken his shot.

And finally . . .

*Go on, tell me, what **would** happen if that rabbit ran off with my ball?*

Apart from calling the rabbit some defamatory names you would replace the ball with a substitute and put it in a position near to where it came to rest – without penalty of course.

José María Olázabal has become a highly regarded international competitor and will surely collect some major trophies before too long.

That flaming rabbit!

TECHNIQUE

op American golfer Fuzzy Zoeller once described golf thus, 'Hit it. Find it. Hit it again. Add 'em up.' That is quite a nice and simple way of describing a game of golf. What Fuzzy fails to tell you is that he is not a bad player and consequently he doesn't do a lot of hitting, a lot of finding, and doesn't have much to add up. But his philosophy amply describes the game.

But, if you go on to a golf course without knowing how to hold the club, how to stand, how to swing or which way to aim, then you will be doing a lot of hitting, a lot of finding, and a lot of adding up.

Hopefully we will go part of the way towards helping you reduce those calculations on all three counts. The rest, well that is up to you. And the only way your game will improve after being taught the basics is through practice . . .

The first place to start is with the grip. If you can't hold the club properly then your problems start straight away.

The grip

When you play tennis, badminton or other similar racket sports, you are told to make

Grips

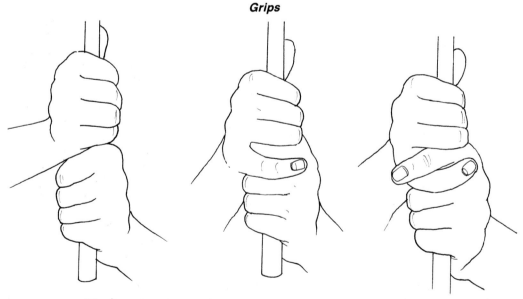

The three basic grips. (Left) the double-handed grip; (centre) the popular Vardon overlapping grip, and (right) the interlocking grip.

HOW · TO · ADOPT
THE · VARDON · GRIP

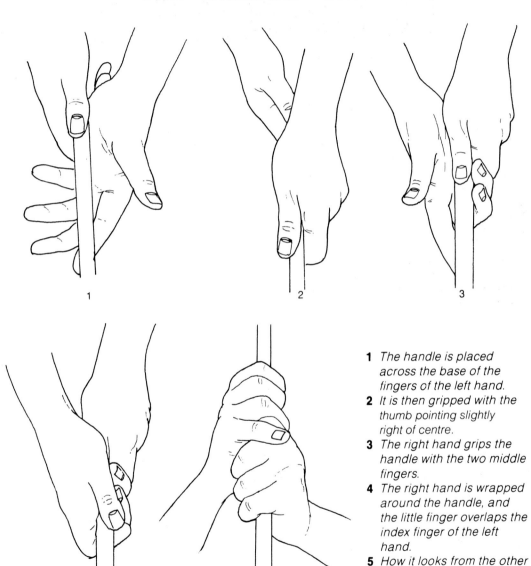

1 The handle is placed across the base of the fingers of the left hand.

2 It is then gripped with the thumb pointing slightly right of centre.

3 The right hand grips the handle with the two middle fingers.

4 The right hand is wrapped around the handle, and the little finger overlaps the index finger of the left hand.

5 How it looks from the other side.

The player can also slip the little finger of the right hand between the index and second finger of the left hand, this is known as the interlocking grip. Players with small hands would be advised to use the full two-handed grip.

sure your grip is comfortable. In golf you will find the first time you grip a club it is far from comfortable and in fact feels awkward . . . if it does feel comfortable then you aren't gripping it properly!

A good grip is vital because it will give you mastery and control of the club, which will reflect in the playing of good, accurate shots.

There are three basic grips: the double-handed grip; the Vardon overlapping grip, named after the legendary Harry Vardon who introduced it; and the interlocking grip.

The Vardon grip is the most popular, but the choice is one only you can make. It is important, however, to make sure that you have a good grip, because without one you will never make a good golfer.

When putting, a different grip is adopted. Players tend to adopt their own putting grip but in most cases they will have both thumbs pointing down the shaft.

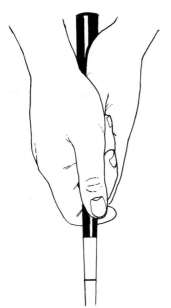

The putting grip

Note how the two thumbs are perpendicular and point down towards the putting surface.

Stance

The stance is the position that you take up when addressing the ball.

There are three types of stance: the square stance; the open stance; and the closed stance.

The stance

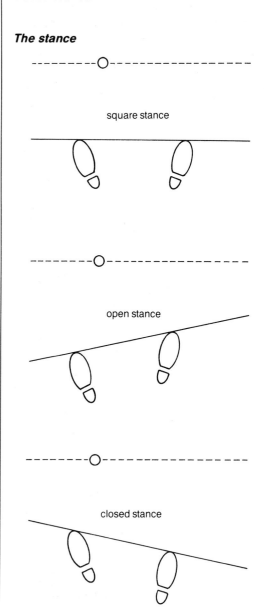

square stance

open stance

closed stance

TECHNIQUE

No matter what stance you adopt you should picture an imaginary line between the ball and the target, that is the line of flight. To take up the square stance your feet will be parallel to the line of flight.

The simple rule to follow when taking up your stance is to position the clubhead behind the ball **before** positioning your feet. The type of club you use will determine your stance. If you are using a driver the ball will be teed up level with your left heel (assuming you are right-handed) and if you are using a wedge the ball will be teed up somewhere between the middle of your feet.

As a general guide, when taking up your stance, your feet should be parallel with your shoulders. However, when using woods your feet will tend to be further apart and with short irons (9-iron, wedge etc.) your feet will be closer together.

If you have the right grip, and have taken up the proper square stance there is no reason why the ball should not follow the intended line of flight if hit correctly. The square stance is adopted when driving from the tee and playing long irons or woods off the fairway.

With an open stance, you bring your left

Flexing your knees

At approach flex your knees slightly, and, most importantly, relax.

foot back from the line of flight. The result of this will see the ball set off to the left before veering right to the intended target. The open stance is adopted when playing approach shots to the green or if your ball is lying in a bad position (in deep rough, etc.).

The closed stance is the opposite. The right foot is drawn back from the line of flight and the ball will first travel to the right before turning in left towards the intended target.

If you are playing from a square stance position and find that your ball is going to the right or left (slicing or hooking), don't try altering your stance – there is every chance that it is your grip that is wrong, and we'll look at those problems a little later. But if you are having these problems, first of all look at your line of fire, and look where your feet are positioned – the two may well not be parallel. Many novices make the mistake of **thinking** they are aiming the ball at the target when in fact it is being aimed well away from it.

No matter what stance you adopt you should slightly bend your legs at the knees and make sure your legs are not too far apart, or too close together. The general rule of thumb is: *the longer the shot, the further apart your feet need to be.*

Never overreach for a ball, and never stand too close to it. A good way of testing if you are standing the right distance from the ball is to place the handle of the club on your left thigh just above the knee after taking up your position. If it rests there comfortably, then you are standing in a good position.

Swing

There is a great deal to get right before you actually play your first shot – you will no doubt have gathered that already, I'm sure. But now we come to the swing.

You have to address the ball, take the clubhead back above and behind your head, bring it back down again and make sure it is back in the same place as it was when you started to take it away from the

The golf swing

1 Address.   *2 Halfway back*   *3 Top of backswing.*

The plane of the swing

The path of the club should follow the same plane on both the backswing and downswing.

4 Downswing.

5 Contact.

6 Follow-through. Eyes should be looking towards the target at the end of the follow-through.

ball. It sounds easy, but in the second or two it takes to carry out the manoeuvre, a lot can happen, and the clubhead only needs to be a fraction out when making contact with the ball and oops! – all sorts of problems can occur.

From the moment you take the clubhead away from the ball to the moment it comes back down to the same point, the club must travel in an arc. The backswing and downswing must follow the same path along that arc. The angle of the arc is called the

plane and is determined by (a) the club used, and (b) your own height. If you can picture Ian Woosnam using a driver he would require a flat plane, whereas Nick Faldo playing a wedge would require an upright plane.

The number one rule in the golf swing is keep your left arm straight (assuming you are right-handed). The left arm should be regarded as an extension of your club.

As you take the clubhead away from the ball and start your backswing you do not

Putting styles

move your feet, and you do not take your eyes off the ball. Your hips swivel as the club goes back and your left shoulder dips under your chin. Halfway through the backswing your wrists should cock and thus enable the club to be parallel with the ground. At this point the body movement will have shifted your weight onto your right foot. As you bring the club down (the downswing) the weight starts to shift to the left leg and the right knee bends inwards. At all times you must keep your head still, and even after making contact with the ball don't be tempted to lift your head to see where the ball has gone. Allow your club to carry on for the follow-through. As it does follow through your head will be lifted automatically.

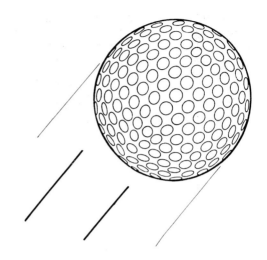

Putting

Putting has been the saviour or destroyer of many a player over the years, whether he be a club player or a leading professional. You can salvage a series of poor approach shots by sinking a great putt to complete the hole, or you can destroy great approach play by taking three, or even four or more putts.

Putting is the one aspect of golf that takes a long time to master. For a start, all greens have their own peculiarities. There are so many factors which influence how a green plays: weather conditions, when a green was last cut, and the placement of the hole are all examples. Even the greens on your own course can vary from day to day. They may be fast one day, they may be slow the next. The ability to 'read' a green comes with experience. You are well advised to spend ten minutes or so on the practice greens before you start a round. They will give you some idea how the main greens are playing.

To try and tell you how to putt would be wrong. If I went into great length about putting technique you would then sit in front of your television, watch all the world's great players and see not two with the same putting style. That is how specialist and individual putting is. It is up to you to develop your own putting style.

As a guideline, you must remember that the putting stroke comes from the arm and the top half of the trunk. The rest of the body remains perfectly still. Once you have lined up your putt the clubhead must be brought away from the ball gently and the ball stroked, not hit, towards the hole.

Being able to successfully 'read a green' is what makes a good putter. You must look for any undulations or notice whether the green slopes to the right or left, or is it an uphill or downhill putt. Remember, it is always easier to putt uphill than downhill so, if a green has a noticeable slope on it, you need to play your approach shot to the green so that your ball lands on the bottom half of it.

If you have a long putt, say the full length of the green, you need to visualize a 3ft (1m) circle around the hole and make it your goal to get the ball into that circle. If the ball goes in the hole it is then a bonus. If it doesn't then you stand a chance of getting your second putt in.

As we said earlier, the putting grip is different to other grips. Your thumbs should be on the top of the handle and be pointing towards the putting surface.

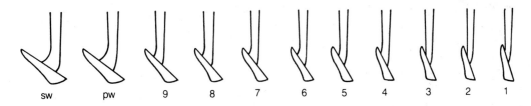

sw   pw   9   8   7   6   5   4   3   2   1

Which club to use?

This diagram shows how the loft of the irons varies, affecting the flight and distance that may be obtained with each . . . assuming the ball is hit correctly by a first class player.

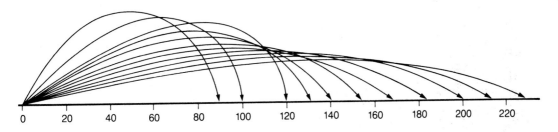

0   20   40   60   80   100   120   140   160   180   200   220

What club to use and when

For long drives off the tee a wood is generally used. But having said that, you will see many professionals these days using long irons (1-iron) from the tee. More accuracy can be obtained with an iron than a wood, but greater distance can be obtained with the wood, particularly the driver.

However, if you are using your wood off the tee, you are well advised to start learning with your 2- or 3-wood before experimenting with the driver. It is a difficult club to get used to.

Once on the fairway you have to assess the distance to the green, wind conditions, and general weather conditions before making your choice of club. Wind affects the choice of club more than anything. I have

played the same shot on successive visits to the same course that have one day required a 7-iron and on another day a 1-iron, or even a wood. There is no sense in taking something like a 5-iron and hoping to run it along the ground to the green when conditions underfoot are soaking. In a case like this you would be better playing a lofted club, a 9-iron or wedge, and getting the ball to pitch on the green.

So you see, it is impossible to tell you what club to use. The diagram will give you some idea of the length a good player would get with each club, and in normal conditions. But don't forget, these are only to act as a guideline.

However, as a simple guide, and assuming perfect weather conditions (obviously at the Fantasy Island Golf Club), we will play a few

The West German star Bernhard Langer, a calm, undemonstrative character and probably the most consistent of leading players in recent years.

GOLF

Hypothetical situation (1)

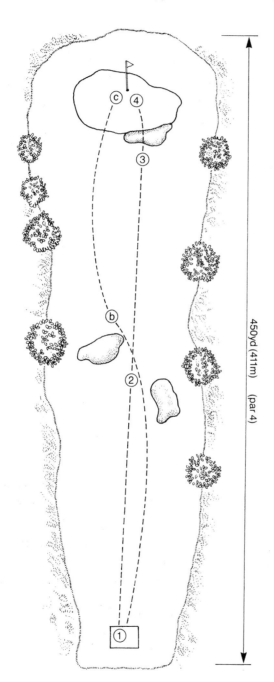

450yd (411m)   (par 4)

Shot 1:
2 iron (trying to gain more accuracy and also playing short of the left-hand bunker).

Shot 2:
3/4 iron, just short of the green.

Shot 3:
pitching wedge ... over bunker.

Shot 4:
putter.

The professional or low handicapped player would play a driver to (b), and then a 4, 5 or 6 iron with fade to (c), straight into the heart of the green.

Hypothetical situation (2)

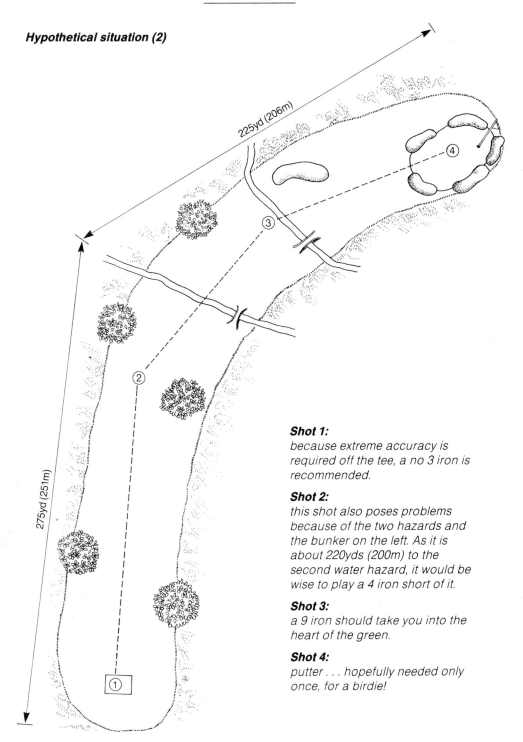

225yd (206m)

275yd (251m)

Shot 1:
because extreme accuracy is required off the tee, a no 3 iron is recommended.

Shot 2:
this shot also poses problems because of the two hazards and the bunker on the left. As it is about 220yds (200m) to the second water hazard, it would be wise to play a 4 iron short of it.

Shot 3:
a 9 iron should take you into the heart of the green.

Shot 4:
putter . . . hopefully needed only once, for a birdie!

holes and give an indication what club would be used. But please, only regard it as a guide. I cannot legislate how much power you can put into a ball – and that's another thing: you can play a shot with the same club either with full power or just half-hit. The path of the ball will be the same but its distance will, naturally, vary. It is worth remembering that you may see a shot as a 7-iron, when a half-played 5-iron would do the job just as well, or vice-versa.

The slice

One of the most common faults in golf is slicing the ball to the right of its intended target (for right-handed players). The slice can occur because the ball is positioned too far forward, but the most common reason for the slice is a poor grip, often as a result of the right hand coming too far over the left hand, or the left hand going too far round to the left of the club handle. Because the grip is wrong the path of the clubhead will not be true on its return to the ball when striking. It will come across the ball with the face open and put

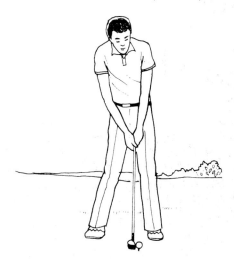

A triumphant Nick Faldo of England, winner of the 1987 British Open at Turnberry, holding the game's greatest trophy aloft.

The slice

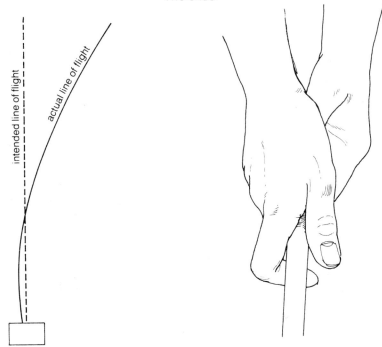

intended line of flight

actual line of flight

If you are slicing, look at your grip . . . it most probably looks like this. If it does, move your right hand anti-clockwise (as you look at it), slightly more under the handle of the club.

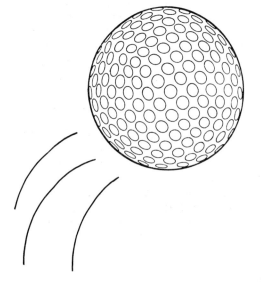

sidespin on it. After leaving the club the ball will go to the left slightly and the spin will then take it out to the right. To cure the slice look at your grip. I'm sure you will find that that is where the problem lies.

The hook

Just as infuriating as the slice is the hook, where the ball veers to the left of its intended target. Positioning the ball too far back at address can be a problem but again, you are well advised to look at your grip. This time you will most probably find your hands are over to the right of the handle too much. The hook is again caused by the sidespin put on the ball.

The hook

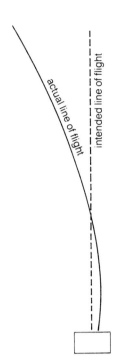

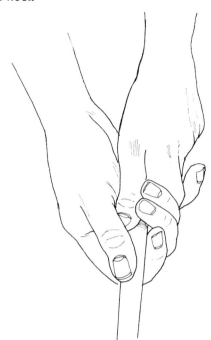

Hooking? A sloppy grip like this could be the problem . . . look at the thumbs – they are pointing in different directions. The left thumb should be slightly to the right of centre, and the right thumb slightly left.

Playing uphill or downhill shots

Never easy to play, the most common fault when playing uphill or downhill shots is the tendency to lean into, or away, from the slope of the hill . . . **don't**. In both cases, set your stance at right angles to the ground. Consequently the club will be allowed to complete its follow through after making contact with the ball and will not be hit into the ground. When playing uphill the ball will have extra loft on it, consequently a longer club than normal will have to be chosen. When playing downhill it is advisable to position the ball more towards the back foot than normal.

If you are playing on the side of a hill and the ball is either above or below your feet you should, if playing with the ball above your feet, move your hands slightly down the handle and lean slightly forward into the shot. The spin imparted on the ball will take it to the left of its intended target, so you need to aim to the right.

If the ball is below the level of your feet you need to lean forward, but this time as far as you can . . . without falling over. Because of your position and that of the ball, the spin of the ball will take it to the right, so you need to aim to the left of your target.

Whatever you do, don't rush the shot. There is often a tendency to hurry an awkward shot, in the hope that it will be over and done with more quickly; don't!

PLAYING · ON · SLOPES

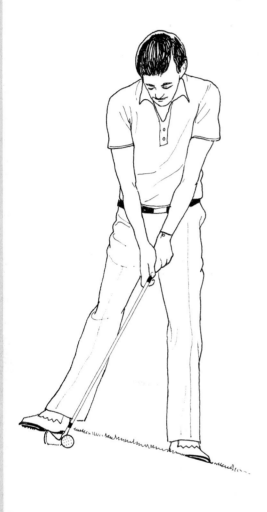

Playing downhill: Note where the feet are positioned in relation to the ball, and the left arm is parallel with the right leg. And those eyes are firmly fixed on the ball . . .

Playing uphill: This time the right arm is parallel with the left leg. Note how the left arm forms an extension of the club.

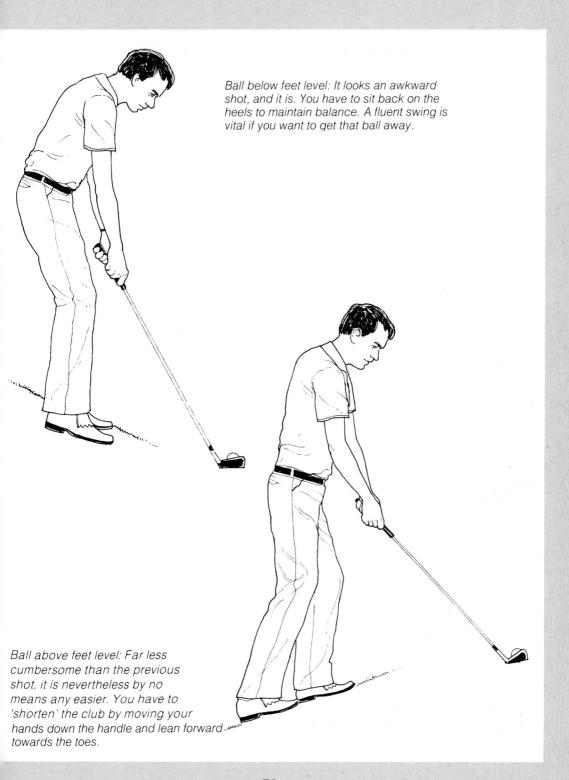

Ball below feet level: It looks an awkward shot, and it is. You have to sit back on the heels to maintain balance. A fluent swing is vital if you want to get that ball away.

Ball above feet level: Far less cumbersome than the previous shot, it is nevertheless by no means any easier. You have to 'shorten' the club by moving your hands down the handle and lean forward towards the toes.

Pitching and chipping

Pitching is carried out with either a pitching wedge or, a sand-iron. The pitch is a lofted shot close to the green which is normally played in order to clear an obstacle – a bunker, bush, or something like that. To play the pitch an open stance is adopted and the feet brought closer together. The club is held down the handle and the swing is slowed down. Because only a short distance is normally covered with a pitch, the club doesn't need to be brought back with a full backswing.

Chipping is also done when the ball is near to the green but a lofted club is not necessary. You may have no obstruction between you and the hole. You could therefore chip the ball to the green by using a 6- or 7- iron. The club should again be gripped down the handle and the stance very narrow. The ball should be positioned level with the right foot, and doesn't need a lot of flight. Once it lands on the green it will run up to the hole.

Getting out of bunkers

The first thing to remember about bunker play is **you are not allowed to ground your club** before making the shot.

The normal grip is adopted but a very open stance is taken up. The sand wedge is used but it does not make contact with the ball, it hits the sand, about 1in (2.54cm) behind the ball. The sand will then propel the ball in an upward motion and, hopefully, onto the green. It is very important that you follow-through as fully as you would with any normal shot off the tee or from the fairway. The ball needs all the help it can get out of a bunker! Don't forget to smooth over your footprints as you leave the bunker.

Playing out of a bunker

Note how open the stance is. Contact is not made with the ball, but with the sand about 1in (3cm) behind the ball.

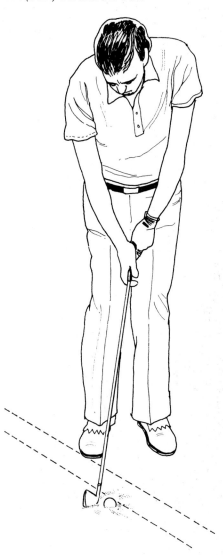

Nick Price follows the flight of his fairway shot. The Zimbabwean has begun to achieve good international wins after years of narrowly failing in the big championships.

GOLF

That's about it. I've told you how to play the basic golf strokes. Like any sport, practice is all-important in golf. You will find golf a frustrating game at times; you can play a magnificent drive from the tee straight down the fairway and, just as you are feeling good and thinking 'What's all the fuss about? This is easy', you will then slice a 7-iron into deep rough and lose your ball.

Golf is like that, but more importantly, it is a great game, and one you will enjoy.

As a newcomer to the game, the most frustrating aspect you will encounter is your inability to play what appear to be easy shots with consistency. The great players make it look all too simple, and that is why they are great. However, the beauty of golf is that you don't have to be a great player to enjoy the game. It is a great leveller, as you will soon find out. thanks to the handicap system, you can enjoy a game against players better than yourself. In fact, you will find that playing with better players will improve your game.

A round of golf can take anything up to four hours, and sometimes even longer, but go out and enjoy it. Whatever you do, respect the golf course. It has taken years to develop, but it only takes a short time for it to be ruined. It has been put there for your benefit, so enjoy it, and don't forget to treat it with respect. Having said that, believe me, it will have no respect for you!

Have fun . . !

Jose-Maria Canizares of Spain, playing out of a bunker during a Ryder Cup match in 1985. Canizares is a top European golfer and, together with Ballesteros, Pinero and Olazabal, has made Spain one of the world's leading golf nations.

USEFUL
ADDRESSES

Council of National Golf Unions
Formby Golf Club
Golf Road
Formby
L37 1LQ
Tel: 071 487 2164

English Golf Union
1–3 Upper King Street
Leicester
LE1 6XF

English Schools' Golf Association
20 Dykenooke Close
Whickham
Newcastle-upon-Tyne
NE16 5DT
Tel: 091 488 3538

European Golf Association
69 Avenue Victor Hugo
75783 Paris 16
France

Golf Foundation
Foundation House
Hanbury Manor
Ware
Hertfordshire
SG12 0UH
Tel: 0920 484044

Golfing Union of Ireland
Glencar House
81 Eglinton Road
Donnybrook
Dublin 4
Eire
Tel: 010 3531 269411

Ladies' Golf Union
The Scores
St Andrews
Fife
Scotland
KY16 9AT
Tel: 0334 75811

Professional Golfers Association
Sandy Jones, Executive Director
PGA Headquarters
Apollo House
The Belfry
Sutton Coldfield
West Midlands B76 9PT

PGA European Tour
Wentworth Club
Wentworth Drive
Virginia Water
Surrey GU25 4LS

USEFUL · ADDRESSES

Royal and Ancient Golf Club
St Andrews
Fife
Scotland KY16 9JD

Scottish Golf Union
The Cottage
181a Whitehouse Road
Barnton
Edinburgh EH4 6BY
Tel: 031 339 7546

Scottish Schools' Golf Association
Leith Academy
20 Academy Park
Edinburgh
Scotland
Tel: 031 554 0606

Welsh Golfing Union
Powys House
Cwmbran
Gwent
NP44 1PB
Tel: 0633 870261

Welsh Schools' Golf Association
c/o Mr G. White
King Henry VIII School
Abergavenny
Gwent
NP7 6EP
Tel: 0873 852701

Women Professional Golfers' European Tour
The Tytherington Club
Macclesfield
Cheshire
SK10 2JP
Tel: 0625 611444

United States Golf Association
Golf House
PO Box 708
Far Hills
New Jersey 07931-0708
USA
Tel: 201 234 2300

RULES CLINIC

INDEX

The Daly Drive! John Daly winds up in preparation for launching another spectacular drive during the 1993 British Open where, as ever, this big hitter drew a huge gallery of support for each of his rounds.

INDEX